Twinkle Verses

SHANMATHI SRIRAMULU

ISBN 979-8-89026-704-7

Contents

❖ CONTENTS ❖

Foreword

The author Ms. Shanmathi.S, M.A., M.Phil., is working as the Lecturer in the Department of English at Dr. M.G.R. Government Arts and Science College for Women, Villupuram. She is pursuing Ph.D., in Joseph Arts & Science College, Thirunavalur. She has a good experience in teaching students. She has a flair for teaching English. I am extremely happy to note that she is publishing a book consisting of 25 poems with different titles. In this book she has proved her mettle to cope well with her teaching responsibilities and as a poet. Her poems deal with a wide range of social issues, contemporary issues faced by the mankind and about nature. She has her own pattern of writing as a poet; many of the poems in the first few lines create an interest and curiosity among the readers to go further to get to know the subject which she wanted to highlight. I am sure that this young Indian woman poet has a long way to go and eventually emerge as an established and popular poet for her works.

My best wishes.

Dr. D. Ganesan
Principal
Dr. M.G.R Govt Arts and
Science College for Women,
Villupuram,
Tamil Nadu.

It's really a pleasant experience to read the Poems of Poet Shanmathi. She has delved deep into various themes of current interest splendidly in her poems. She takes us on a journey of intimate details concerning nature and natural objects, love - hate relationships, day-to-day life events and many more interesting topics. She has touched upon every aspect of human life with her mesmerizing magical words.

For instance, she has pulled inspiration from the natural world and finds healing from Mother Nature: "Like a don/the Sun waves it's dawn/... slimy shining snakes swallowed the frogs like snacks... (The Hungry Hostellers of Earth). In the poem "Do you know who am I?" she throws a fresh insight about crow's life: I sit and talk/with our flock/I'm not crucially chained/I'm not terribly trained/I go wherever/and eat whatever.

Poet Shanmathi never fails to highlight the aping of western lifestyle that has a deadly impact on our richest indigenous culture, customs and family values: "Baked foods blames the cooked food/Shrunken skirts and shirts slays sarees!.../Even after the sunset/the impact of colonization/utterly spreads its infection on humans...(Modest Murder). She surprises us with her play of imagination that is pleasing to our senses. She is deeply aware of the injustices around her in society. Some of the poems like "Modest Murder", "Paradise Shop", "Loveless Ritual" reflect her social consciousness and responsibility.

Her impactful poems invite multiple visitations giving fresh insights to the readers. She deserves our utmost praise and adoration. According to Shelley, a great poem is a fountain forever overflowing with waters of wisdom and delight. Verily her elegant poems amalgamate both. She has made a difference, a delightful difference. A difference that's delightful to the heart and soul. Her distinct voice will be heard through ages.

Dr. L. Ravi Shankar
Principal,
Government Arts and Science College,
Thirukovilur.

Pen and Paper

Whenever I try to sculpture reality
in my verse,
my mighty sword disguised as a pen
falls in love with a plain paper
and keeps kissing her with his nib.
Without hesitation, she blushed in ink.

Her blank space tempts my pen
by exposing her unkissed parts.
Their sensuous love preached to me:
The fusion of his sharpness and her purity
is beyond human love.
I understood them as made for each other.

Explanation

Whenever an author tries to write something, the pen falls in love with the plain paper. The writing process is denoted as the kisses of nib. Just like a woman the paper also blushed and changed its colour out of shyness. Here, the pen's sharpness refers to a man and the paper's purity refers to a woman.

The Quarrelling Queens

The Moon came in delight
After twilight,
Stars jumped with glitter
Echoed a cheerful twitter
Their minds are mounted with cold war
To attain the prestigious queenly power.

Stars claimed their infinity
as the majority.
The Moon asserted her brightness
as highness.
Stars felt proud for being touched by no man
The Moon proved that she was the favourite of humans.

Envy and Wrath flamed their fury
To meet the Dark Sky Jury.
Dark sky smirked "Stars and Glow-worm
can never stand firm for long-term.
The Moon may be a universal beauty
but her life span is unfit for stable duty".

Neither stars nor the Moon
The jury played a new tune.
The Dark sky declared herself as the queen
for being a big black background screen
making these quarrellers visible
and following the principle of invisible.

Hearing this comic case of his co-staff
The Sun came to the scene with a sarcastic laugh.
When this hero of the day arrived high,
the quarrelling queens left with shy.

Explanation

The moon and the stars came after the sunset. "Who is the real queen of night?", is the only quarrel between them. The stars boasted about its majority in numbers and the Moon felt pride of being everyone's favourite. The Jealous and Anger made them meet the judge Dark sky for an impartial judgement. Surprisingly, the Dark Sky declared herself as the queen and stated, these Stars and the Moon are visible because of her dark background. With a sarcastic laughter, when the Sun came up like a hero, the quarrelling queens left.

Flatterers

'A lonely woman' is a feast
for those who starved like a beast.
Women are sold like a caged dove
in the name of Love,
flatterers fly like falcon
and type text like Bacon.
To satisfy their hunger
or to extinguish their anger
merciless men utilize women
only to hit her hymen.
He migrates his mood from plate to plate
after the date with his mate.

Explanation

In the name of love, women are betrayed and sold like a commodity around the world. Some men make use of the chance when they find a woman lonely. They try to impress women with their art of writing and speaking. He tries to sacrifice anything until she accepts him. They satisfy their physical pleasures and move towards another woman.

Modest Murder

Is that true?
The westernization implanted
Its delusions of grandeur over people
like a Buccaneer,
and interrupting our culture like beetles.

Yes, it's true.
Eras drowned, some corporate seagulls
erasing our tradition
to conquer our identity,
following the map of Macaulay.

Is that true?
Even after the Sunset,
the impact of colonization
utterly spread its infection on humans
with a fantasy for modernization?

Yes, it's true.
Baked food blames the cooked food!...
Shrunken skirts and shirts slay sarees!...
Allopathic medicine avoids Ayurveda!...
Modernity murders our culture modestly.

Explanation

The westerners attracted Indians with their carefree culture. Once, Lord Babington Macaulay said, culture and tradition is the backbone of India, the colonizers can rule only if they break the pattern. Some loyal corporates of Macaulay, still trying to erase the Indian tradition and custom. India became Independent, but the modern culture of westerners infected the Indian minds. Cooked food is seen as unhealthy and half-baked food as branded. The Indian sarees are replaced by short skirts and shirts. English medicines interrupted Indian medicines. Modernity murders Indian culture modestly.

Deadly Love

At first blush
Your essence of bravery
Whispered your victory
And defeated my ambush.

Your patriotic vigilance
Possessed me to possess your heart,
I wafted away my soul from captive
To surrender beneath your shoulder.

Despite the enmity in between
Our green and saffron country
We were united
In the war field.

With a ridiculous hope of love
When I hugged my secret soldier's heart
My knight knelt down like a groom
Married me, even though I'm a **BULLET**.

Explanation

Love at first sight. The bullet's shyness was defeated by the soldier's bravery and victory. His patriotism possessed the bullet, she absconded from her own country out of love to surrender under the control of soldier. Despite the war between two countries, she united with him on the battlefield. When the bullet captured the knight's heart, he knelt down like a groom and accepted it bravely.

Do You Know Who Am I?

I am not a Parrot
Forced to repeat for a carrot
I am not a Peacock
Being hunted for a huge lock
I am not a Love bird
Arrested and admired for whirred
I am not a Goose
Shot to serve as a fleshy spicy juice
I am not an Eagle
Who lands rarely like a regal.

I sit and talk
With our flock
I am not crucially chained
I am not terribly trained
I go wherever
And eat whatever
We eat Mutton at mosque,
Taste the temple feast
And cakes at cathedral
I am proud of being a **CROW**.

Make-Up of a Mrs.

Is there anyone aware
        what her foundation says?
All guessed
        she is battling with her brightness.
No,
   it hides her sorrow face.

Is there anyone aware
        what her lipstick says?
All guessed,
        her lusty lips
                may lock all the lapses!
Only she knew how
        it fantasies a fake smile!

Is there anyone aware
        what her 'concealer' says?
All guessed,
        she veils her complexion.
In reality, she covers her swollen eyes.
Make up of a real Mrs.
is to really make herself up.

Explanation

When a married woman grooms herself, it does not mean that she wants to attract other men. Sometimes, at some places a woman's character is being misjudged based on her makeup. Her makeup veils her scars and wounded face of her distress life. She applied foundation to brighten her dull face. Her lipstick coated lips silenced her laments with a fake smile. Her concealer covers her swollen eyes. So do not judge a woman's makeup.

The Memorable Militants

Sons of our Incredible Indian soil
born out of our mighty motherland,
defends our nation with a belief:
"Protecting my motherland
is safeguarding my women and children"
They never worked for salary hikes
They sincerely serve for their society
They run,
      They hide,
            They battle,
They are mad to be medalled as martyrs!

The Hushed Hall

When some clouds found me insecure
without an umbrella,
they chased me like a criminal
until I got shelter
under a well-furnished roof.

I admired men and women there
soaked in a peaceful world
enjoyed one another's company.
This enchanting spot encouraged me
to sign up as a new member among them.

Some pleased in pleasure,
some sank in somber.
This venue rehabilitates and resurrects
the frustrated feelings of few
and introduces a new man each day.

One soothed me philosophically,
One proposed me poetically,
One wondered me about war,
One satirized the powerful politicians,
One voiced out against Injustice.

Aristotle, Wordsworth, Tolstoy,
Orwell, Tagore, Karl Marx
Kafka and many,
my poverty prohibited me
to have them all, as my own.

I extravagantly spend my hours
engaging them
and dropping them on time
in the shelves of the hushed hall
'the library'.

Explanation

The dark clouds chased the poetess every nook and corner, at last she took shelter under a great place called library. There she found men and women spending their time peacefully. It tempted her to enrol herself as a new member among them. Some books present happiness and some shatter the spirit, it is a home of rehabilitation or resurrection. Library is the place where dead authors give solutions to living people. The poetess favoured the fortune of reading all philosophers, poets, historians and satirists in one library. Here, in the library, the poor poetess spends more time and engages herself with all authors.

Sleep

Yes, I am intoxicated
for octa hours
whenever I am frustrated,
to rejuvenate my verse with empirical powers.

Whoever believed to be born with currency bills,
spilling suit cases of shilling
to buy this sleep in the form of pills,
in order to escape from unnecessary yelling.

Some students got trapped in it,
misdirected to the kingdom of idle.
One who intakes it with a limit will always benefit
One who drowned himself, may lose his goal's vital.

So enlighten your lantern of destiny with sleep.
Give life to your dreams even if you fall **ASLEEP.**

Explanation

The society in which we are living, people spending suit cases of shilling(money) to buy a peaceful sleep. They beg doctors to prescribe sleeping tablets, in order to escape their sleepless nights. Students who sleep anytime, never succeed. Students having limited sleep will always benefit. The poetess herself intoxicates eight hours of sleep to make her mind fresh. A sound sleep is the best source of energy for our dreams to get life.

The Harmless Weapon

God created Men

Men magnified Religion

Religion welcomed Caste

Caste accepted Discrimination

Discrimination boosted Chauvinists

Chauvinists branded some as Untouchables

Untouchables were chased towards Marginalization

Marginalization made them to erupt against the elite exploiters

Elite exploiters have been challenged by the scheduled with a harmless weapon

The harmless weapon is called EDUCATION.

Paradise Shop

This fallacy of paradise
fantasized men prior
Now flattering female with entice,
to derive pleasure out of their desire.

On those days, it was sited
at the outskirts, not inside the town.
Men felt guilty to go there uninvited
and left before the Moon comes down.

Men and Women hang out with glass
in this twenty first century
are praised as upper class,
very soon getting pictured in the obituary.

Alcoholics advertise this paradise shop
called 'Wine shop'.

Explanation

Once upon a time, alcohol attracted only men, at present, even women are getting addicted. On those days, men felt shy to enter the wine shop, they tried to finish up their business and return before everyone woke up. The bar was located at the outskirts. In the twenty-first century, whoever hangs out with glasses is praised as the upper class. The elite culture turned some men and women as alcoholics and helped them to get pictured in the obituary. They advertise wine shops as a paradise.

Cry of an Answer Script

Right or wrong,
neat or ugly,
my benevolent bare body blushed
when students sketched stories!
and shaded with solutions!
My transparency is tortured by touches,
teacher's ticks tickled me
I'm an intellect!
I'm an idiot!
I'm an average!
Why am I being valued for someone?
I'M NOT WHAT I'M...

The Secret Shell

Sometimes I overhear sweet voices

deep down the dark den and rejoices

I strained to overcome the sense of being dumb

however, all my hum goes numb.

I am blind, to mind

good or bad of mankind.

I enjoyed my feast

when she ate like a beast.

Day by day, week by week

there's a growth in my physique.

I desired to disconnect from her clutch

and dared to descend, to get in touch.

If she is my Thetis*

I am blessed to be her Foetus.

* THETIS - Mother of warrior Achilles, persuaded her son to fight in the Trojan war even though she knows Achilles will die in that war. She wanted her son to be a part of history.

Explanation

The foetus inside the womb can hear the sweet voices outside and strains to speak out loud. He tries to prove that he is vigil inside, unfortunately no parent is blessed with the opportunity to hear their foetus' voice. He accepts to stay blind, instead of finding good and bad among humans. Whatever food the mother consumed, the foetus inside enjoyed it like a feast. When the foetus fully grew up, he wanted to get rid of her womb and to get in touch with his mother. Every child believes that his mother is the only strongest woman in the world.

Love in the Time of Summer

I stood for days and weeks
to solemnize my soul.
His ebbs made my day blooming,
his flows withered my world.
Some despised him for being obnoxious
some believed, he conquests the cold
The universe baptized my hero "THE SUN"
The enlightening lantern of celestial tower
I declare myself as the Sun's Lover
My name is Sunflower

Loveless Ritual

'She broke my heart', you blamed
You cried, 'She left me deserted'
The pain has stabbed you untamed
and even bewitched your life diverted.

Threatened by the power of caste
she smashed all your chances to fight
and avoided a massive religious blast
which would have slain you like a kite.

She struggled to shatter her father's prophecy
of getting you slaughtered,
to avoid all the discrepancy
in their conservative clan being tattered.

She burnt your unbreakable love
and handcuffed by a loveless wedding now.

Explanation

The man cried and blamed that his beloved broke his heart and left him deserted. The pain made him wild and diverted his life. Since the man's beloved was threatened by the power of caste, she was not ready to give him a chance. She wanted to safeguard him. When she realized her father's hatred towards her lover, she buried him deep inside her heart and married a man without love.

The God's Handmade

The voice of breeze echoed
in the hills and valleys
introduced me their allies
as God's handmade.

The roaring rocky shores
    Migrating moonlight
        Shimmering sunlight
            Green grassy floor beneath the doors
                The aroma of colourful blossoms
                    Decently dressed bushy trees
                        Sight of streaky lightning strikes
                            Delicious kisses of drizzling and many
Wisely warned me, 'walk out from windows!'
Calmly convinced me, 'come in contact with our allies'
Neutrally nurtured me, 'Nature is Natural'.

My Infected Lines

The disloyal of many
Is a Distilled honey
One who wedded the grudge
Never obeys a judge.
Some do not respect some
Due to the demand of sum.
Pessimists spread like a mist
And arrest the optimist like a blacklist.
These infected lines
Burst out like mines.

Explanation

Never believe a disloyal person, their relationship fades like a distilled honey. One who holds the revenge will never look into morals or justice. People started to trust that the value of money has become more valuable than being human. A person is respected on the basis of his wealth. Instead of being positive and good, everyone started supporting the pessimistic attitude. These are social infections spreading everywhere. It really hurts to see a society becoming materialistic. When you experience this kind of bad infection, you will burst out like mine.

A Poetess' Cupid

A cupid
     who inspired a poetess,
       long lives in literature.
Through her literary spell of immortality.
Her love makes love to diction
And gives birth to virgin verses.

Her verse praises the love of her prince
Who bestowed her the crown of poetess
To define their calm love.
She wrote,
     writes
       and will write
Until she becomes an asset to death!

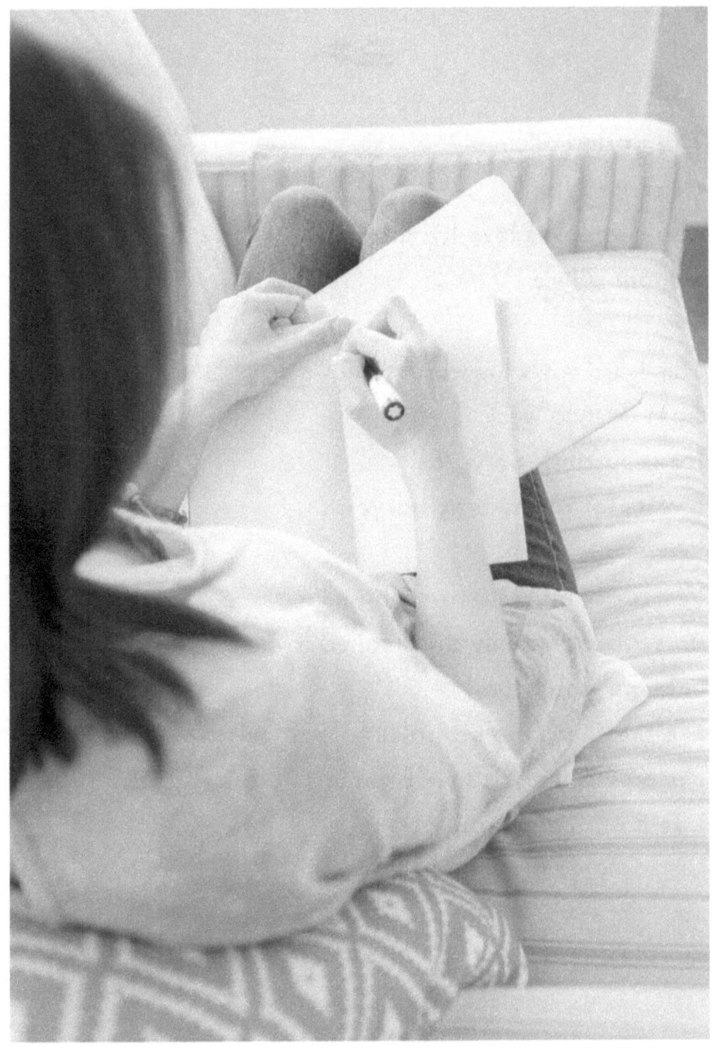

Is He a Poet?

The world calls him
a licensed liar
who composes love hymns
without a lyre.

This bard sows his words
from east to west,
for thousands of 'yards'
awaits for a romantic harvest.

Yes, a poet is a literary physician
prescribes the only drug called love
in his prescription,
like the One who scribbles fate above.
His only saying 'If love conquests all,
Life can rule overall'.

Butterfly Kisses

You travelled around oceans
Like an Albatross
In search of his mate.

I craved for your scent
Like a child praying for his gift
From Santa.

The touch of your hands
Lifted my toes like a Ballet dancer
Out of coyness.

Our eyes fenced to and fro
You deliberately defeated my eyelids
With your butterfly kisses.

The Hungry Hostellers of Earth

Like a Don
the Sun waved its dawn,
Decomposers displayed a show of shrubs
dancing salsa when the Sun stood.
Like food safety inspectors,
the insects inspected the taste of shrubs.
Fully formed frogs filled their tummy with insects!
Slimy shining snakes swallowed the frogs like snacks!
Hungry hawks are honoured with their snake hunt!
At last the left out decomposes.
The earth is a hostel for every creature
they stay
till their span ends,
they vacate
when their cycle ends.

Explanation

When the Sun rises, the food cycle starts. All the living beings on earth wake up to enjoy its day. Shrubs peeped up with the support of decomposers. The insects tasted the shrubs. Frogs filled up their stomachs with the insects. Those frogs are swallowed by snakes. Hawks hunt the snakes and leave its stool to become decomposers. The food chain is continuing with the same methodology for centuries, but not with the same species. Every creature stays like a hosteller on the earth until their life span ends. No species is allowed to stay forever. Nothing is permanent in this world.

The Moon's Vengeance

Darkened dusk daily deletes the day
and acclaims its authority until AM.
To court the conduct of my country men,
the mesmerizing Moon makes her "moon walk"
by leaving a luxurious lusty look.

I, the poor poetess portraying the perfection
of sensuous sight of the Sirius star,
missed the majestic moon in my manuscript.
She hooked the handsome heart of my hero
out of revenge.

A Confession

Love of my life
I Promised to be your wife
and flew far away from you
without leaving any clue!
I lost my way
and became a hunter's prey.
I survive,
There's no chance to revive
You misjudged my present, perfect,
however, I live like a suspect.
Still, our separation
is crucifying me like cremation.
Here, I confess
for charming you like a sorceress.

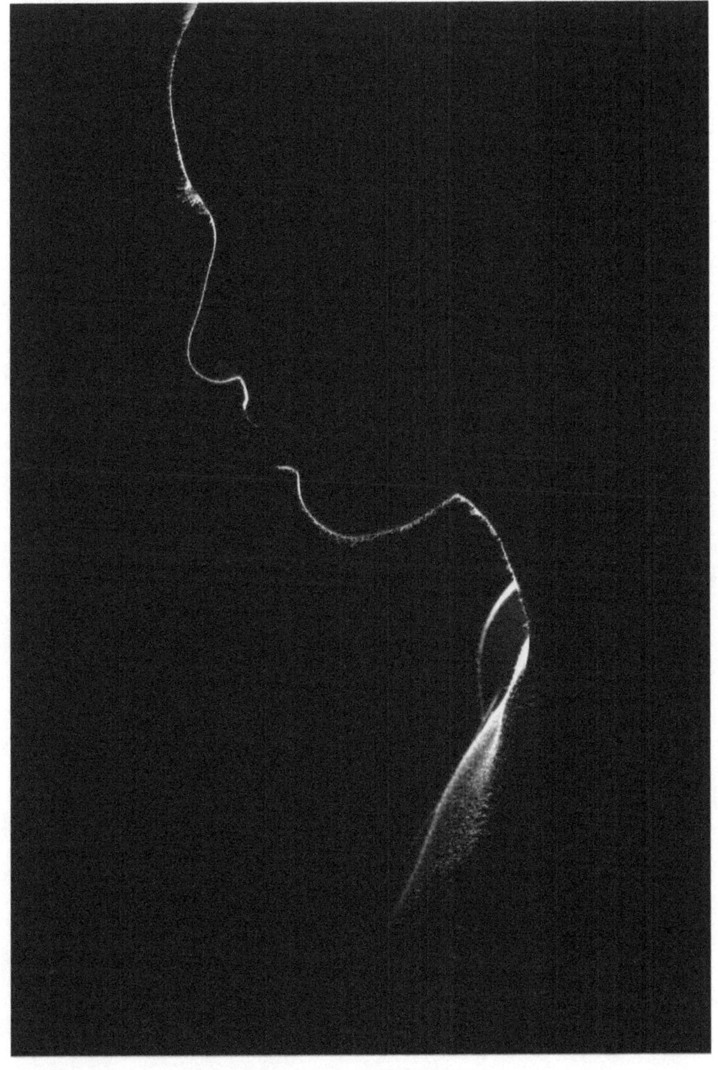

An Apology of a Mother

I beg your pardon,
for always kissing you like a mouth organ.
I beg your pardon,
for over caring you now and then.

Before making you to fall asleep
sometimes, I myself go to deep sleep.
To feed you a spoon
I try my best to fake a tune.

I Apologize
for not allowing you out of my eyes.
I Apologize
for giving you too much advice.
Let's comprise
and chase all our lies like flies.
May our love rise
and make us wise.

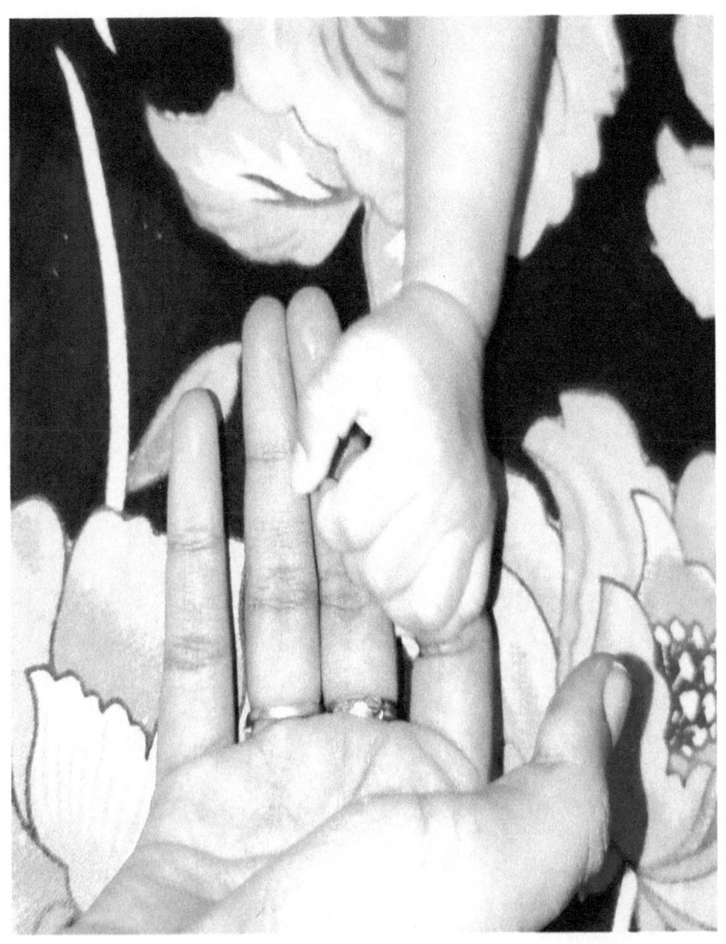